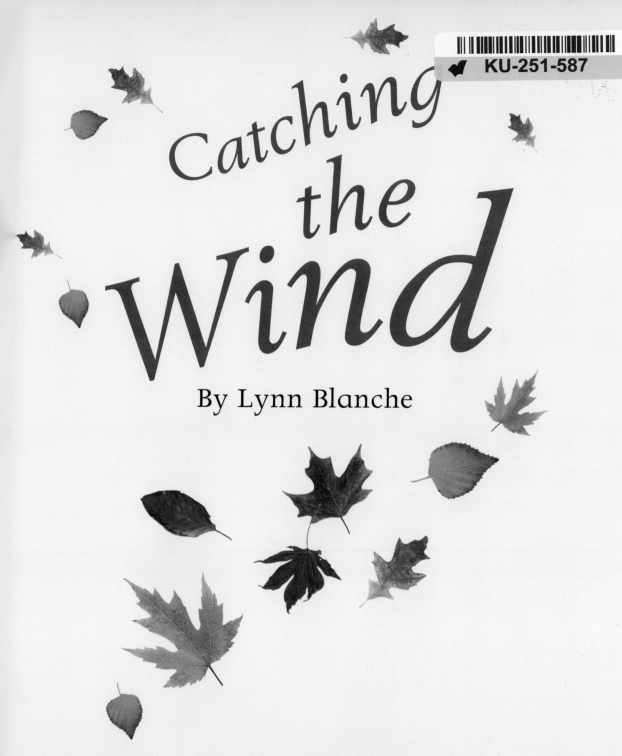

Catching the Wind

By Lynn Blanche

Contents

What Is Wind?

It rattles the windows on a stormy night.
It rustles the leaves on trees. It pushes you
along the street. What is it? It's the wind.

Wind is moving air. You can't see wind, but you can see what it does. Seeds scatter, clothes blow in the breeze and flags flutter.

Wind produces a **force** that moves things. The force of the wind pushes things, making them move. Wind helps lift a kite into the air.

Wind helps a kite to fly.

Wind produces different amounts of force. A soft breeze produces a small force. It blows the seeds off a dandelion. A strong wind produces a large force. It blows huge trees back and forth.

The **Beaufort Scale** measures the strength of the wind. As the wind gets stronger, the numbers get bigger. The scale also shows what can happen when winds of different strengths blow.

The Beaufort Scale

0 Smoke rises straight up.

1 Smoke drifts.

2 Leaves sway.

3 Flags flutter.

4 Paper flies.

5 Medium waves form.

6 Umbrellas turn inside out.

7 Walking is hard.

8–9 Roof tiles blow off.

10–11 Trees fall.

12 Buildings fall.

Wind Helps Boats Move

Wind helps sailing boats move through water. Sometimes the wind pulls on the sail. Other times it blows across the sail. A sailor moves the sail to catch the wind to move the boat.

Long ago ships carried people and cargo
to many countries. Ships often had many sails
to catch the wind. But, if the wind didn't blow,
the ships didn't move.

In the 1800s ships like this
carried tea around the world.

Today many boats don't have to count on wind power alone. They also have engines. If the wind dies, then engine power can move the boat along.

Wind Helps People Work

Long ago people used big stones to grind grain into flour. Turning the heavy stones was hard work. Later people built windmills to turn the stones.

It often took two people to grind grain into flour.

Windmills were invented hundreds of years ago.

Parts of a Windmill

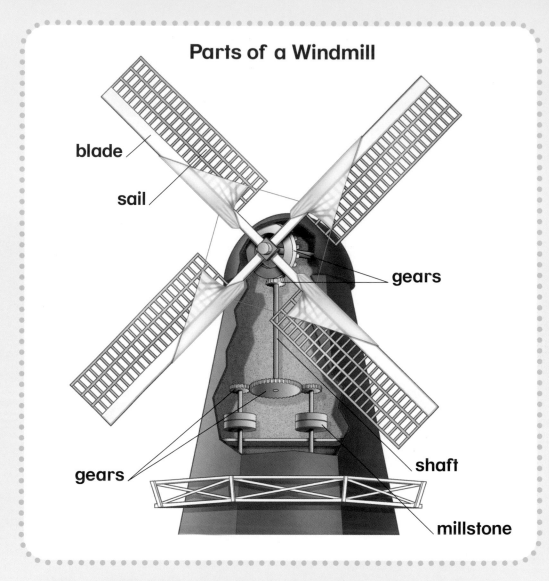

How did a windmill work? The wind blew on the sails and turned the blades. The blades were connected to a shaft and gears. When they turned, so did the **millstones**.

Today windmills still grind grain in some places. People also use **wind turbines**. They use wind power to make **electricity**. This electricity is used to run many different machines.

Wind Farms

Places where many wind turbines work together are called **wind farms**. Wind farms are found in very windy places. Many are on flat fields.

Too Much Wind

Sometimes wind power is dangerous.
Strong winds break tree branches,
knock down fences and cause huge waves.
Tornadoes and **hurricanes** uproot trees,
send cars flying and even flatten houses.

Still, wind isn't always dangerous. People use wind to fly kites, hang glide, sail and windsurf. Wind power helps people have fun!

Glossary

Beaufort Scale   a scale used to measure
                     wind power

electricity   a kind of energy that makes
                     machines and lights work

force   a push or pull that moves things

hurricanes   powerful storms that form
                     over warm water

millstones   big stones used to grind grain
                     into flour

tornadoes   powerful windstorms shaped
                     like twisting, spinning funnels
                     that form mostly over land

wind farms   places where a number of wind
                     turbines are grouped together

wind turbines   tall towers with large, spinning
                     blades that are used to make
                     electricity